Scripture Memory MAP

FOR WOMEN

A CREATIVE JOURNAL

BARBOUR BOOKS
An Imprint of Barbour Publishing, Inc.

Published by Barbour Books, an imprint of Barbour Publishing, Inc., 1810 Barbour Drive, Uhrichsville, Ohio 44683, www.barbourbooks.com

Our mission is to inspire the world with the life-changing message of the Bible.

 Member of the
Evangelical Christian
Publishers Association

Printed in China.

What Does Scripture Memory Look Like?

Get ready to commit God's Word to heart with this creative journal, where every colorful page will guide you to create your very own scripture memory map—by writing out specific goals, thoughts, and ideas that you can follow from start to finish—as you begin your scripture memorization journey. (Be sure to record the date on each one of your scripture memory maps so you can look back over time and track what you've learned!)

The Scripture Memory Map for Women not only will encourage you to spend time focusing on and thinking about the life-changing truths of God's Word but also will help you build a healthy spiritual habit of Bible memorization for life!

Don't know where to begin? Check out the helpful list of recommended Bible memory verses at the back of this book!

Date:

MY MEMORY VERSE FOR TODAY:

....
....
....
....
....

THIS VERSE IS IMPORTANT TO REMEMBER BECAUSE. . .

....
....
....
....
....
....

WHAT IT MEANS TO MY FAITH:

....
....
....
....
....

KNOWING THIS VERSE WILL BE HELPFUL WHEN. . .

MY PRAYER FOR TODAY:

*I have stored up your word in my heart,
that I might not sin against you.*

PSALM 119:11 ESV

Date:

MY MEMORY VERSE FOR TODAY:

....
....
....
....
....

THIS VERSE IS IMPORTANT TO REMEMBER BECAUSE. . .

....
....
....
....
....
....

WHAT IT MEANS TO MY FAITH:

....
....
....
....
....

KNOWING THIS VERSE WILL BE HELPFUL WHEN. . .

MY PRAYER FOR TODAY:

There's nothing like the written Word of God for showing you the way to salvation through faith in Christ Jesus. Every part of Scripture is God-breathed and useful one way or another— showing us truth, exposing our rebellion, correcting our mistakes, training us to live God's way. Through the Word we are put together and shaped up for the tasks God has for us.

2 Timothy 3:16–17 MSG

Date:

MY MEMORY VERSE FOR TODAY:

....

....

....

....

....

THIS VERSE IS IMPORTANT TO REMEMBER BECAUSE. . .

....

....

....

....

....

WHAT IT MEANS TO MY FAITH:

....

....

....

....

....

HOW IT APPLIES TO MY LIFE:

....

....

....

....

KNOWING THIS VERSE WILL BE HELPFUL WHEN. . .

....

....

....

....

....

MY PRAYER FOR TODAY:

....

....

....

....

....

....

*They delight in the law of the LORD, meditating on it
day and night. They are like trees planted along the riverbank,
bearing fruit each season. Their leaves never wither,
and they prosper in all they do.*

PSALM 1:2–3

Date:

MY MEMORY VERSE FOR TODAY:

....

....

....

....

....

THIS VERSE IS IMPORTANT TO REMEMBER BECAUSE. . .

....

....

....

....

....

WHAT IT MEANS TO MY FAITH:

....

....

....

....

....

HOW IT APPLIES TO MY LIFE:

....

....

....

....

KNOWING THIS VERSE WILL BE HELPFUL WHEN. . .

....

....

....

....

....

MY PRAYER FOR TODAY:

....

....

....

....

....

....

*"When I discovered your words, I devoured them.
They are my joy and my heart's delight, for I bear
your name, O LORD God of Heaven's Armies."*

JEREMIAH 15:16

Date:

MY MEMORY VERSE FOR TODAY:

....

....

....

....

....

THIS VERSE IS IMPORTANT TO REMEMBER BECAUSE. . .

....

....

....

....

....

....

WHAT IT MEANS TO MY FAITH:

....

....

....

....

....

HOW IT APPLIES TO MY LIFE:

....

....

....

....

KNOWING THIS VERSE WILL BE HELPFUL WHEN. . .

....

....

....

....

....

MY PRAYER FOR TODAY:

....

....

....

....

....

....

*"I have not departed from his commands,
but have treasured his words more than daily food."*

JOB 23:12

Date:

MY MEMORY VERSE FOR TODAY:

....

....

....

....

....

THIS VERSE IS IMPORTANT TO REMEMBER BECAUSE. . .

....

....

....

....

....

WHAT IT MEANS TO MY FAITH:

....

....

....

....

KNOWING THIS VERSE WILL BE HELPFUL WHEN. . .

MY PRAYER FOR TODAY:

Write these commandments that I've given you today on your hearts. Get them inside of you and then get them inside your children. Talk about them wherever you are, sitting at home or walking in the street; talk about them from the time you get up in the morning to when you fall into bed at night. Tie them on your hands and foreheads as a reminder; inscribe them on the doorposts of your homes and on your city gates.

DEUTERONOMY 6:6–9 MSG

Date:

MY MEMORY VERSE FOR TODAY:

....

....

....

....

....

THIS VERSE IS IMPORTANT TO REMEMBER BECAUSE. . .

....

....

....

....

....

WHAT IT MEANS TO MY FAITH:

....

....

....

....

....

HOW IT APPLIES TO MY LIFE:

....

....

....

....

KNOWING THIS VERSE WILL BE HELPFUL WHEN. . .

....

....

....

....

....

MY PRAYER FOR TODAY:

....

....

....

....

....

....

*"And the seeds that fell on the good soil represent honest,
good-hearted people who hear God's word, cling to it,
and patiently produce a huge harvest."*

LUKE 8:15

Date:

MY MEMORY VERSE FOR TODAY:

....

....

....

....

....

THIS VERSE IS IMPORTANT TO REMEMBER BECAUSE. . .

....

....

....

....

....

WHAT IT MEANS TO MY FAITH:

....

....

....

....

....

HOW IT APPLIES TO MY LIFE:

....

....

....

....

KNOWING THIS VERSE WILL BE HELPFUL WHEN. . .

....

....

....

....

....

MY PRAYER FOR TODAY:

....

....

....

....

....

....

....

*"We live by every word that comes
from the mouth of the LORD."*

DEUTERONOMY 8:3

Date:

MY MEMORY VERSE FOR TODAY:

....
....
....
....
....

THIS VERSE IS IMPORTANT TO REMEMBER BECAUSE. . .

....
....
....
....
....

WHAT IT MEANS TO MY FAITH:

....
....
....
....
....

HOW IT APPLIES TO MY LIFE:

....

....

....

....

KNOWING THIS VERSE WILL BE HELPFUL WHEN. . .

....

....

....

....

....

MY PRAYER FOR TODAY:

....

....

....

....

....

....

*Don't copy the behavior and customs of this world,
but let God transform you into a new person by changing
the way you think. Then you will learn to know God's
will for you, which is good and pleasing and perfect.*

ROMANS 12:2

Date:

MY MEMORY VERSE FOR TODAY:

....

....

....

....

....

THIS VERSE IS IMPORTANT TO REMEMBER BECAUSE. . .

....

....

....

....

....

WHAT IT MEANS TO MY FAITH:

....

....

....

....

HOW IT APPLIES TO MY LIFE:

....

....

....

....

KNOWING THIS VERSE WILL BE HELPFUL WHEN. . .

....

....

....

....

....

MY PRAYER FOR TODAY:

....

....

....

....

....

....

....

*Wise words are more valuable
than much gold and many rubies.*

PROVERBS 20:15

Date:

MY MEMORY VERSE FOR TODAY:

....

....

....

....

THIS VERSE IS IMPORTANT TO REMEMBER BECAUSE. . .

....

....

....

....

....

WHAT IT MEANS TO MY FAITH:

....

....

....

....

....

HOW IT APPLIES TO MY LIFE:

....

....

....

....

KNOWING THIS VERSE WILL BE HELPFUL WHEN. . .

....

....

....

....

....

MY PRAYER FOR TODAY:

....

....

....

....

....

For if you listen to the word and don't obey, it is like glancing at your face in a mirror. You see yourself, walk away, and forget what you look like. But if you look carefully into the perfect law that sets you free, and if you do what it says and don't forget what you heard, then God will bless you for doing it.

JAMES 1:23–25

Date:

MY MEMORY VERSE FOR TODAY:

....

....

....

....

....

THIS VERSE IS IMPORTANT TO REMEMBER BECAUSE. . .

....

....

....

....

....

WHAT IT MEANS TO MY FAITH:

....

....

....

....

HOW IT APPLIES TO MY LIFE:

....

....

....

....

KNOWING THIS VERSE WILL BE HELPFUL WHEN. . .

....

....

....

....

....

MY PRAYER FOR TODAY:

....

....

....

....

....

....

....

So we must listen very carefully to the truth
we have heard, or we may drift away from it.

HEBREWS 2:1

Date:

MY MEMORY VERSE FOR TODAY:

....

....

....

....

....

THIS VERSE IS IMPORTANT TO REMEMBER BECAUSE. . .

....

....

....

....

....

WHAT IT MEANS TO MY FAITH:

....

....

....

....

....

HOW IT APPLIES TO MY LIFE:

KNOWING THIS VERSE WILL BE HELPFUL WHEN. . .

MY PRAYER FOR TODAY:

*Listen carefully to my wisdom; take to heart what
I can teach you. You'll treasure its sweetness deep within;
you'll give it bold expression in your speech.*

PROVERBS 22:17–18 MSG

Date:

MY MEMORY VERSE FOR TODAY:

....
....
....
....
....

THIS VERSE IS IMPORTANT TO REMEMBER BECAUSE. . .

....
....
....
....
....

WHAT IT MEANS TO MY FAITH:

....
....
....
....
....

HOW IT APPLIES TO MY LIFE:

....

....

....

....

KNOWING THIS VERSE WILL BE HELPFUL WHEN. . .

....

....

....

....

....

MY PRAYER FOR TODAY:

....

....

....

....

....

....

....

I will study your commandments
and reflect on your ways.
PSALM 119:15

Date:

MY MEMORY VERSE FOR TODAY:

....

....

....

....

....

THIS VERSE IS IMPORTANT TO REMEMBER BECAUSE. . .

....

....

....

....

....

....

WHAT IT MEANS TO MY FAITH:

....

....

....

....

....

HOW IT APPLIES TO MY LIFE:

....

....

....

....

KNOWING THIS VERSE WILL BE HELPFUL WHEN. . .

....

....

....

....

....

MY PRAYER FOR TODAY:

....

....

....

....

....

....

....

You will keep in perfect peace all who trust in you,
all whose thoughts are fixed on you!

ISAIAH 26:3

Date:

MY MEMORY VERSE FOR TODAY:

....
....
....
....
....

THIS VERSE IS IMPORTANT TO REMEMBER BECAUSE. . .

....
....
....
....
....

WHAT IT MEANS TO MY FAITH:

....
....
....
....
....

HOW IT APPLIES TO MY LIFE:

....

....

....

....

KNOWING THIS VERSE WILL BE HELPFUL WHEN. . .

....

....

....

....

....

MY PRAYER FOR TODAY:

....

....

....

....

....

....

For the word of God is alive and powerful. It is sharper than the sharpest two-edged sword, cutting between soul and spirit, between joint and marrow. It exposes our innermost thoughts and desires.

HEBREWS 4:12

Date:

MY MEMORY VERSE FOR TODAY:

....

....

....

....

....

THIS VERSE IS IMPORTANT TO REMEMBER BECAUSE. . .

....

....

....

....

....

WHAT IT MEANS TO MY FAITH:

....

....

....

....

....

HOW IT APPLIES TO MY LIFE:

....

....

....

....

KNOWING THIS VERSE WILL BE HELPFUL WHEN. . .

....

....

....

....

....

MY PRAYER FOR TODAY:

....

....

....

....

....

....

....

"Make them holy by your truth;
teach them your word, which is truth."

JOHN 17:17

Date:

MY MEMORY VERSE FOR TODAY:

....

....

....

....

....

THIS VERSE IS IMPORTANT TO REMEMBER BECAUSE. . .

....

....

....

....

....

....

WHAT IT MEANS TO MY FAITH:

....

....

....

....

....

....

....

....

....

KNOWING THIS VERSE WILL BE HELPFUL WHEN. . .

....

....

....

....

....

MY PRAYER FOR TODAY:

....

....

....

....

....

....

"Give in to God, come to terms with him and
everything will turn out just fine. Let him
tell you what to do; take his words to heart."

JOB 22:21–22 MSG

Date:

MY MEMORY VERSE FOR TODAY:

....

....

....

....

....

THIS VERSE IS IMPORTANT TO REMEMBER BECAUSE. . .

....

....

....

....

....

WHAT IT MEANS TO MY FAITH:

....

....

....

....

....

HOW IT APPLIES TO MY LIFE:

....

....

....

....

KNOWING THIS VERSE WILL BE HELPFUL WHEN. . .

....

....

....

....

....

MY PRAYER FOR TODAY:

....

....

....

....

....

....

....

I honor and love your commands.
I meditate on your decrees.

PSALM 119:48

Date:

MY MEMORY VERSE FOR TODAY:

....
....
....
....
....

THIS VERSE IS IMPORTANT TO REMEMBER BECAUSE. . .

....
....
....
....
....
....

WHAT IT MEANS TO MY FAITH:

....
....
....
....
....

HOW IT APPLIES TO MY LIFE:

....

....

....

....

KNOWING THIS VERSE WILL BE HELPFUL WHEN. . .

....

....

....

....

....

MY PRAYER FOR TODAY:

....

....

....

....

....

....

*Fix your thoughts on what is true, and honorable,
and right, and pure, and lovely, and admirable. Think
about things that are excellent and worthy of praise.*

PHILIPPIANS 4:8

Date:

MY MEMORY VERSE FOR TODAY:

....

....

....

....

....

THIS VERSE IS IMPORTANT TO REMEMBER BECAUSE. . .

....

....

....

....

....

....

WHAT IT MEANS TO MY FAITH:

....

....

....

....

....

HOW IT APPLIES TO MY LIFE:

KNOWING THIS VERSE WILL BE HELPFUL WHEN. . .

MY PRAYER FOR TODAY:

*"You must commit yourselves wholeheartedly
to these commands that I am giving you today."*

DEUTERONOMY 6:6

Date:

MY MEMORY VERSE FOR TODAY:

....

....

....

....

....

THIS VERSE IS IMPORTANT TO REMEMBER BECAUSE. . .

....

....

....

....

....

WHAT IT MEANS TO MY FAITH:

....

....

....

....

....

HOW IT APPLIES TO MY LIFE:

....

....

....

....

KNOWING THIS VERSE WILL BE HELPFUL WHEN. . .

....

....

....

....

....

MY PRAYER FOR TODAY:

....

....

....

....

....

....

*My child, pay attention to what I say. Listen
carefully to my words. Don't lose sight of them.
Let them penetrate deep into your heart.*

PROVERBS 4:20–21

Date:

MY MEMORY VERSE FOR TODAY:

....
....
....
....
....

THIS VERSE IS IMPORTANT TO REMEMBER BECAUSE. . .

....
....
....
....
....

WHAT IT MEANS TO MY FAITH:

....
....
....
....
....

KNOWING THIS VERSE WILL BE HELPFUL WHEN. . .

MY PRAYER FOR TODAY:

*Let the word of Christ dwell in you richly, teaching
and admonishing one another in all wisdom,
singing psalms and hymns and spiritual songs,
with thankfulness in your hearts to God.*

COLOSSIANS 3:16 ESV

Date:

MY MEMORY VERSE FOR TODAY:

....

....

....

....

....

THIS VERSE IS IMPORTANT TO REMEMBER BECAUSE. . .

....

....

....

....

....

....

WHAT IT MEANS TO MY FAITH:

....

....

....

....

....

HOW IT APPLIES TO MY LIFE:

....

....

....

....

KNOWING THIS VERSE WILL BE HELPFUL WHEN. . .

....

....

....

....

....

MY PRAYER FOR TODAY:

....

....

....

....

....

....

....

*Your word is a lamp to guide my
feet and a light for my path.*

PSALM 119:105

MY MEMORY VERSE FOR TODAY:

THIS VERSE IS IMPORTANT TO REMEMBER BECAUSE. . .

WHAT IT MEANS TO MY FAITH:

HOW IT APPLIES TO MY LIFE:

....

....

....

....

KNOWING THIS VERSE WILL BE HELPFUL WHEN. . .

....

....

....

....

....

MY PRAYER FOR TODAY:

....

....

....

....

....

....

....

*Be a good worker, one who does not need to be ashamed
and who correctly explains the word of truth.*

2 TIMOTHY 2:15

Date:

MY MEMORY VERSE FOR TODAY:

....

....

....

....

....

THIS VERSE IS IMPORTANT TO REMEMBER BECAUSE. . .

....

....

....

....

....

WHAT IT MEANS TO MY FAITH:

....

....

....

....

....

HOW IT APPLIES TO MY LIFE:

....

....

....

....

KNOWING THIS VERSE WILL BE HELPFUL WHEN. . .

....

....

....

....

....

MY PRAYER FOR TODAY:

....

....

....

....

....

....

....

....

I will delight in your decrees and not forget your word.

PSALM 119:16

Date:

MY MEMORY VERSE FOR TODAY:

....

....

....

....

....

THIS VERSE IS IMPORTANT TO REMEMBER BECAUSE. . .

....

....

....

....

....

WHAT IT MEANS TO MY FAITH:

....

....

....

....

....

HOW IT APPLIES TO MY LIFE:

....

....

....

....

KNOWING THIS VERSE WILL BE HELPFUL WHEN. . .

....

....

....

....

....

MY PRAYER FOR TODAY:

....

....

....

....

....

....

*"So commit yourselves wholeheartedly to these
words of mine. Tie them to your hands and
wear them on your forehead as reminders."*

DEUTERONOMY 11:18

Date:

MY MEMORY VERSE FOR TODAY:

....

....

....

....

....

THIS VERSE IS IMPORTANT TO REMEMBER BECAUSE. . .

....

....

....

....

....

WHAT IT MEANS TO MY FAITH:

....

....

....

....

....

HOW IT APPLIES TO MY LIFE:

....

....

....

....

KNOWING THIS VERSE WILL BE HELPFUL WHEN. . .

....

....

....

....

....

MY PRAYER FOR TODAY:

....

....

....

....

....

....

....

Your laws are wonderful.
No wonder I obey them!

PSALM 119:129

Date:

MY MEMORY VERSE FOR TODAY:

....

....

....

....

....

THIS VERSE IS IMPORTANT TO REMEMBER BECAUSE. . .

....

....

....

....

....

WHAT IT MEANS TO MY FAITH:

....

....

....

....

....

KNOWING THIS VERSE WILL BE HELPFUL WHEN. . .

MY PRAYER FOR TODAY:

Never let loyalty and kindness leave you! Tie them around your neck as a reminder. Write them deep within your heart. Then you will find favor with both God and people, and you will earn a good reputation.

PROVERBS 3:3–4

Date:

MY MEMORY VERSE FOR TODAY:

....

....

....

....

....

THIS VERSE IS IMPORTANT TO REMEMBER BECAUSE. . .

....

....

....

....

....

....

WHAT IT MEANS TO MY FAITH:

....

....

....

....

....

HOW IT APPLIES TO MY LIFE:

KNOWING THIS VERSE WILL BE HELPFUL WHEN. . .

MY PRAYER FOR TODAY:

*Those who love your instructions have
great peace and do not stumble.*

PSALM 119:165

Date:

MY MEMORY VERSE FOR TODAY:

....

....

....

....

....

THIS VERSE IS IMPORTANT TO REMEMBER BECAUSE. . .

....

....

....

....

....

WHAT IT MEANS TO MY FAITH:

....

....

....

....

....

HOW IT APPLIES TO MY LIFE:

....

....

....

....

KNOWING THIS VERSE WILL BE HELPFUL WHEN. . .

....

....

....

....

....

MY PRAYER FOR TODAY:

....

....

....

....

....

....

*Do not forget my teaching, but let your heart keep
my commandments, for length of days and years
of life and peace they will add to you.*

PROVERBS 3:1–2 ESV

Date:

MY MEMORY VERSE FOR TODAY:

....

....

....

....

....

THIS VERSE IS IMPORTANT TO REMEMBER BECAUSE. . .

....

....

....

....

....

WHAT IT MEANS TO MY FAITH:

....

....

....

....

....

HOW IT APPLIES TO MY LIFE:

....

....

....

....

KNOWING THIS VERSE WILL BE HELPFUL WHEN. . .

....

....

....

....

....

MY PRAYER FOR TODAY:

....

....

....

....

....

....

"The LORD has declared today that you are his people,
his own special treasure, just as he promised."

DEUTERONOMY 26:18

Date:

MY MEMORY VERSE FOR TODAY:

....

....

....

....

....

THIS VERSE IS IMPORTANT TO REMEMBER BECAUSE. . .

....

....

....

....

....

WHAT IT MEANS TO MY FAITH:

....

....

....

....

....

HOW IT APPLIES TO MY LIFE:

....
....
....
....

KNOWING THIS VERSE WILL BE HELPFUL WHEN. . .

....
....
....
....
....

MY PRAYER FOR TODAY:

....
....
....
....
....
....

You have been taught the holy Scriptures from childhood,
and they have given you the wisdom to receive the
salvation that comes by trusting in Christ Jesus.

2 TIMOTHY 3:15

Date:

MY MEMORY VERSE FOR TODAY:

....
....
....
....
....

THIS VERSE IS IMPORTANT TO REMEMBER BECAUSE. . .

....
....
....
....
....

WHAT IT MEANS TO MY FAITH:

....
....
....
....
....

HOW IT APPLIES TO MY LIFE:

....

....

....

....

KNOWING THIS VERSE WILL BE HELPFUL WHEN. . .

....

....

....

....

....

MY PRAYER FOR TODAY:

....

....

....

....

....

....

*"Study this Book of Instruction continually.
Meditate on it day and night so you will be sure to
obey everything written in it. Only then will you
prosper and succeed in all you do."*

JOSHUA 1:8

Date:

MY MEMORY VERSE FOR TODAY:

....
....
....
....
....

THIS VERSE IS IMPORTANT TO REMEMBER BECAUSE. . .

....
....
....
....
....
....

WHAT IT MEANS TO MY FAITH:

....
....
....
....

HOW IT APPLIES TO MY LIFE:

....

....

....

....

KNOWING THIS VERSE WILL BE HELPFUL WHEN. . .

....

....

....

....

....

MY PRAYER FOR TODAY:

....

....

....

....

....

....

*Trust in the LORD with all your heart; do not depend on
your own understanding. Seek his will in all you do,
and he will show you which path to take.*

PROVERBS 3:5–6

Date:

MY MEMORY VERSE FOR TODAY:

....
....
....
....
....

THIS VERSE IS IMPORTANT TO REMEMBER BECAUSE. . .

....
....
....
....
....
....

WHAT IT MEANS TO MY FAITH:

....
....
....
....
....

HOW IT APPLIES TO MY LIFE:

....

....

....

....

KNOWING THIS VERSE WILL BE HELPFUL WHEN. . .

....

....

....

....

....

MY PRAYER FOR TODAY:

....

....

....

....

....

Don't worry about anything; instead, pray about everything.
Tell God what you need, and thank him for all he has done.
Then you will experience God's peace, which exceeds anything
we can understand. His peace will guard your hearts
and minds as you live in Christ Jesus.

PHILIPPIANS 4:6–7

Date:

MY MEMORY VERSE FOR TODAY:

....
....
....
....
....

THIS VERSE IS IMPORTANT TO REMEMBER BECAUSE. . .

....
....
....
....
....

WHAT IT MEANS TO MY FAITH:

....
....
....
....
....

KNOWING THIS VERSE WILL BE HELPFUL WHEN. . .

MY PRAYER FOR TODAY:

*"Seek the Kingdom of God above all else, and live
righteously, and he will give you everything you need."*
MATTHEW 6:33

Date:

MY MEMORY VERSE FOR TODAY:

THIS VERSE IS IMPORTANT TO REMEMBER BECAUSE. . .

WHAT IT MEANS TO MY FAITH:

HOW IT APPLIES TO MY LIFE:

....

....

....

....

KNOWING THIS VERSE WILL BE HELPFUL WHEN. . .

....

....

....

....

....

MY PRAYER FOR TODAY:

....

....

....

....

....

....

....

....

"Come back to the LORD and live!"

AMOS 5:6

Date:

MY MEMORY VERSE FOR TODAY:

....

....

....

....

....

THIS VERSE IS IMPORTANT TO REMEMBER BECAUSE. . .

....

....

....

....

....

WHAT IT MEANS TO MY FAITH:

....

....

....

....

....

HOW IT APPLIES TO MY LIFE:

....

....

....

....

KNOWING THIS VERSE WILL BE HELPFUL WHEN. . .

....

....

....

....

....

MY PRAYER FOR TODAY:

....

....

....

....

....

....

....

*"Man shall not live by bread alone, but by every
word that comes from the mouth of God."*

MATTHEW 4:4 ESV

Date:

MY MEMORY VERSE FOR TODAY:

....

....

....

....

....

THIS VERSE IS IMPORTANT TO REMEMBER BECAUSE. . .

....

....

....

....

....

WHAT IT MEANS TO MY FAITH:

....

....

....

....

....

KNOWING THIS VERSE WILL BE HELPFUL WHEN. . .

MY PRAYER FOR TODAY:

*"Be careful to obey all these words that I command you,
that it may go well with you and with your children
after you forever, when you do what is good and
right in the sight of the LORD your God."*

DEUTERONOMY 12:28 ESV

Date:

MY MEMORY VERSE FOR TODAY:

....
....
....
....
....

THIS VERSE IS IMPORTANT TO REMEMBER BECAUSE. . .

....
....
....
....
....

WHAT IT MEANS TO MY FAITH:

....
....
....
....
....

HOW IT APPLIES TO MY LIFE:

....

....

....

....

KNOWING THIS VERSE WILL BE HELPFUL WHEN. . .

....

....

....

....

....

MY PRAYER FOR TODAY:

....

....

....

....

....

....

....

*"Come here and listen to the
words of the LORD your God."*
JOSHUA 3:9 ESV

Date:

MY MEMORY VERSE FOR TODAY:

....
....
....
....
....

THIS VERSE IS IMPORTANT TO REMEMBER BECAUSE. . .

....
....
....
....
....
....

WHAT IT MEANS TO MY FAITH:

....
....
....
....
....

HOW IT APPLIES TO MY LIFE:

....

....

....

....

KNOWING THIS VERSE WILL BE HELPFUL WHEN. . .

....

....

....

....

....

MY PRAYER FOR TODAY:

....

....

....

....

....

....

....

*"But even more blessed are all who hear
the word of God and put it into practice."*

LUKE 11:28

Date:

MY MEMORY VERSE FOR TODAY:

....

....

....

....

....

THIS VERSE IS IMPORTANT TO REMEMBER BECAUSE. . .

....

....

....

....

....

....

WHAT IT MEANS TO MY FAITH:

....

....

....

....

....

HOW IT APPLIES TO MY LIFE:

....

....

....

....

KNOWING THIS VERSE WILL BE HELPFUL WHEN. . .

....

....

....

....

....

MY PRAYER FOR TODAY:

....

....

....

....

....

....

....

Look to God's instructions and teachings! People
who contradict his word are completely in the dark.

ISAIAH 8:20

Date:

MY MEMORY VERSE FOR TODAY:

THIS VERSE IS IMPORTANT TO REMEMBER BECAUSE. . .

WHAT IT MEANS TO MY FAITH:

HOW IT APPLIES TO MY LIFE:

....

....

....

....

KNOWING THIS VERSE WILL BE HELPFUL WHEN. . .

....

....

....

....

....

MY PRAYER FOR TODAY:

....

....

....

....

....

....

....

*"The farmer plants seed by
taking God's word to others."*

MARK 4:14

Date:

MY MEMORY VERSE FOR TODAY:

....

....

....

....

....

THIS VERSE IS IMPORTANT TO REMEMBER BECAUSE. . .

....

....

....

....

....

WHAT IT MEANS TO MY FAITH:

....

....

....

....

....

HOW IT APPLIES TO MY LIFE:

KNOWING THIS VERSE WILL BE HELPFUL WHEN. . .

MY PRAYER FOR TODAY:

But those who obey God's word truly show how completely they love him. That is how we know we are living in him.

1 JOHN 2:5

Date:

MY MEMORY VERSE FOR TODAY:

....

....

....

....

....

THIS VERSE IS IMPORTANT TO REMEMBER BECAUSE. . .

....

....

....

....

....

WHAT IT MEANS TO MY FAITH:

....

....

....

....

....

HOW IT APPLIES TO MY LIFE:

....

....

....

....

KNOWING THIS VERSE WILL BE HELPFUL WHEN. . .

....

....

....

....

....

MY PRAYER FOR TODAY:

....

....

....

....

....

....

*For this is the love of God, that we
keep his commandments. And his
commandments are not burdensome.*

1 JOHN 5:3 ESV

Date:

MY MEMORY VERSE FOR TODAY:

....

....

....

....

THIS VERSE IS IMPORTANT TO REMEMBER BECAUSE. . .

....

....

....

....

....

WHAT IT MEANS TO MY FAITH:

....

....

....

....

....

HOW IT APPLIES TO MY LIFE:

....

....

....

....

KNOWING THIS VERSE WILL BE HELPFUL WHEN. . .

....

....

....

....

....

MY PRAYER FOR TODAY:

....

....

....

....

....

....

....

....

God's word lives in your hearts.

1 JOHN 2:14

Date:

MY MEMORY VERSE FOR TODAY:

....

....

....

....

....

THIS VERSE IS IMPORTANT TO REMEMBER BECAUSE. . .

....

....

....

....

....

WHAT IT MEANS TO MY FAITH:

....

....

....

....

....

HOW IT APPLIES TO MY LIFE:

....

....

....

....

KNOWING THIS VERSE WILL BE HELPFUL WHEN. . .

....

....

....

....

....

MY PRAYER FOR TODAY:

....

....

....

....

....

....

For you have been born again, but not to a life
that will quickly end. Your new life will last forever
because it comes from the eternal, living word of God.

1 PETER 1:23

Date:

MY MEMORY VERSE FOR TODAY:

....

....

....

....

....

THIS VERSE IS IMPORTANT TO REMEMBER BECAUSE. . .

....

....

....

....

....

WHAT IT MEANS TO MY FAITH:

....

....

....

....

....

HOW IT APPLIES TO MY LIFE:

....

....

....

....

KNOWING THIS VERSE WILL BE HELPFUL WHEN. . .

....

....

....

....

....

MY PRAYER FOR TODAY:

....

....

....

....

....

....

*So get rid of all the filth and evil in your lives,
and humbly accept the word God has planted in
your hearts, for it has the power to save your souls.*

JAMES 1:21

Date:

MY MEMORY VERSE FOR TODAY:

....

....

....

....

....

THIS VERSE IS IMPORTANT TO REMEMBER BECAUSE. . .

....

....

....

....

....

WHAT IT MEANS TO MY FAITH:

....

....

....

....

....

HOW IT APPLIES TO MY LIFE:

....

....

....

....

KNOWING THIS VERSE WILL BE HELPFUL WHEN. . .

....

....

....

....

....

MY PRAYER FOR TODAY:

....

....

....

....

....

....

And have you forgotten the encouraging words God spoke to you as his children? He said, "My child, don't make light of the LORD's discipline, and don't give up when he corrects you."

HEBREWS 12:5

Date:

MY MEMORY VERSE FOR TODAY:

....

....

....

....

....

THIS VERSE IS IMPORTANT TO REMEMBER BECAUSE. . .

....

....

....

....

....

WHAT IT MEANS TO MY FAITH:

....

....

....

....

....

HOW IT APPLIES TO MY LIFE:

....

....

....

....

KNOWING THIS VERSE WILL BE HELPFUL WHEN. . .

....

....

....

....

....

MY PRAYER FOR TODAY:

....

....

....

....

....

....

Remember your leaders who taught you the word of God.
Think of all the good that has come from their lives,
and follow the example of their faith.

HEBREWS 13:7

Date:

MY MEMORY VERSE FOR TODAY:

....
....
....
....
....

THIS VERSE IS IMPORTANT TO REMEMBER BECAUSE. . .

....
....
....
....
....

WHAT IT MEANS TO MY FAITH:

....
....
....
....
....

HOW IT APPLIES TO MY LIFE:

....

....

....

....

KNOWING THIS VERSE WILL BE HELPFUL WHEN. . .

....

....

....

....

....

MY PRAYER FOR TODAY:

....

....

....

....

....

....

....

"I delight to do your will, O my God;
your law is within my heart."
PSALM 40:8 ESV

Date:

MY MEMORY VERSE FOR TODAY:

....
....
....
....
....

THIS VERSE IS IMPORTANT TO REMEMBER BECAUSE. . .

....
....
....
....
....

WHAT IT MEANS TO MY FAITH:

....
....
....
....
....

HOW IT APPLIES TO MY LIFE:

....

....

....

....

KNOWING THIS VERSE WILL BE HELPFUL WHEN. . .

....

....

....

....

....

MY PRAYER FOR TODAY:

....

....

....

....

....

....

....

The word of God cannot be chained.

2 TIMOTHY 2:9

MY MEMORY VERSE FOR TODAY:

THIS VERSE IS IMPORTANT TO REMEMBER BECAUSE. . .

WHAT IT MEANS TO MY FAITH:

HOW IT APPLIES TO MY LIFE:

....

....

....

....

KNOWING THIS VERSE WILL BE HELPFUL WHEN. . .

....

....

....

....

....

MY PRAYER FOR TODAY:

....

....

....

....

....

....

*Since everything God created is good, we should not
reject any of it but receive it with thanks. For we know
it is made acceptable by the word of God and prayer.*

1 TIMOTHY 4:4–5

Date:

MY MEMORY VERSE FOR TODAY:

....
....
....
....
....

THIS VERSE IS IMPORTANT TO REMEMBER BECAUSE. . .

....
....
....
....
....
....

WHAT IT MEANS TO MY FAITH:

....
....
....
....

HOW IT APPLIES TO MY LIFE:

....

....

....

....

KNOWING THIS VERSE WILL BE HELPFUL WHEN. . .

....

....

....

....

....

MY PRAYER FOR TODAY:

....

....

....

....

....

....

....

*And now the word of the Lord is ringing
out from you to people everywhere.*

1 THESSALONIANS 1:8

Date:

MY MEMORY VERSE FOR TODAY:

....
....
....
....
....

THIS VERSE IS IMPORTANT TO REMEMBER BECAUSE. . .

....
....
....
....
....

WHAT IT MEANS TO MY FAITH:

....
....
....
....
....

HOW IT APPLIES TO MY LIFE:

....

....

....

....

KNOWING THIS VERSE WILL BE HELPFUL WHEN. . .

....

....

....

....

....

MY PRAYER FOR TODAY:

....

....

....

....

....

....

....

*This God—his way is perfect; the word of the LORD proves
true; he is a shield for all those who take refuge in him.*

PSALM 18:30 ESV

Date:

MY MEMORY VERSE FOR TODAY:

....
....
....
....
....

THIS VERSE IS IMPORTANT TO REMEMBER BECAUSE. . .

....
....
....
....
....

WHAT IT MEANS TO MY FAITH:

....
....
....
....
....

HOW IT APPLIES TO MY LIFE:

....

....

....

....

KNOWING THIS VERSE WILL BE HELPFUL WHEN. . .

....

....

....

....

....

MY PRAYER FOR TODAY:

....

....

....

....

....

....

We never stop thanking God that when you received his message from us, you didn't think of our words as mere human ideas. You accepted what we said as the very word of God—which, of course, it is. And this word continues to work in you who believe.

1 THESSALONIANS 2:13

Date:

MY MEMORY VERSE FOR TODAY:

....

....

....

....

....

THIS VERSE IS IMPORTANT TO REMEMBER BECAUSE...

....

....

....

....

....

WHAT IT MEANS TO MY FAITH:

....

....

....

....

HOW IT APPLIES TO MY LIFE:

....

....

....

....

KNOWING THIS VERSE WILL BE HELPFUL WHEN. . .

....

....

....

....

....

MY PRAYER FOR TODAY:

....

....

....

....

....

....

....

*Put on salvation as your helmet, and take the
sword of the Spirit, which is the word of God.*

EPHESIANS 6:17

Date:

MY MEMORY VERSE FOR TODAY:

....

....

....

....

....

THIS VERSE IS IMPORTANT TO REMEMBER BECAUSE. . .

....

....

....

....

....

WHAT IT MEANS TO MY FAITH:

....

....

....

....

HOW IT APPLIES TO MY LIFE:

....

....

....

....

KNOWING THIS VERSE WILL BE HELPFUL WHEN. . .

....

....

....

....

....

MY PRAYER FOR TODAY:

....

....

....

....

....

....

*We don't try to trick anyone or
distort the word of God.*

2 CORINTHIANS 4:2

Date:

MY MEMORY VERSE FOR TODAY:

....

....

....

....

THIS VERSE IS IMPORTANT TO REMEMBER BECAUSE. . .

....

....

....

....

....

WHAT IT MEANS TO MY FAITH:

....

....

....

....

HOW IT APPLIES TO MY LIFE:

....

....

....

....

KNOWING THIS VERSE WILL BE HELPFUL WHEN. . .

....

....

....

....

....

MY PRAYER FOR TODAY:

....

....

....

....

....

....

....

Trust in the LORD with all your heart,
and do not lean on your own understanding.
PROVERBS 3:5 ESV

Date:

MY MEMORY VERSE FOR TODAY:

....

....

....

....

....

THIS VERSE IS IMPORTANT TO REMEMBER BECAUSE. . .

....

....

....

....

....

WHAT IT MEANS TO MY FAITH:

....

....

....

....

....

HOW IT APPLIES TO MY LIFE:

....

....

....

....

KNOWING THIS VERSE WILL BE HELPFUL WHEN. . .

....

....

....

....

....

MY PRAYER FOR TODAY:

....

....

....

....

....

....

....

*"Anyone who belongs to God listens
gladly to the words of God."*

JOHN 8:47

Date:

MY MEMORY VERSE FOR TODAY:

....

....

....

....

....

THIS VERSE IS IMPORTANT TO REMEMBER BECAUSE. . .

....

....

....

....

....

WHAT IT MEANS TO MY FAITH:

....

....

....

....

HOW IT APPLIES TO MY LIFE:

....

....

....

....

KNOWING THIS VERSE WILL BE HELPFUL WHEN. . .

....

....

....

....

....

MY PRAYER FOR TODAY:

....

....

....

....

....

....

....

....

"For the word of God will never fail."

LUKE 1:37

Date:

MY MEMORY VERSE FOR TODAY:

....

....

....

....

....

THIS VERSE IS IMPORTANT TO REMEMBER BECAUSE. . .

....

....

....

....

....

WHAT IT MEANS TO MY FAITH:

....

....

....

....

....

HOW IT APPLIES TO MY LIFE:

....

....

....

....

KNOWING THIS VERSE WILL BE HELPFUL WHEN. . .

....

....

....

....

....

MY PRAYER FOR TODAY:

....

....

....

....

....

....

....

The grass withers, the flower fades,
but the word of our God will stand forever.
ISAIAH 40:8 ESV

Date:

MY MEMORY VERSE FOR TODAY:

....
....
....
....
....

THIS VERSE IS IMPORTANT TO REMEMBER BECAUSE. . .

....
....
....
....
....

WHAT IT MEANS TO MY FAITH:

....
....
....
....
....

HOW IT APPLIES TO MY LIFE:

....

....

....

....

KNOWING THIS VERSE WILL BE HELPFUL WHEN. . .

....

....

....

....

....

MY PRAYER FOR TODAY:

....

....

....

....

....

....

....

"You search the Scriptures because you think they give you eternal life. But the Scriptures point to me!"

JOHN 5:39

Date:

MY MEMORY VERSE FOR TODAY:

....
....
....
....
....

THIS VERSE IS IMPORTANT TO REMEMBER BECAUSE. . .

....
....
....
....
....
....

WHAT IT MEANS TO MY FAITH:

....
....
....
....
....

HOW IT APPLIES TO MY LIFE:

....

....

....

....

KNOWING THIS VERSE WILL BE HELPFUL WHEN. . .

....

....

....

....

....

MY PRAYER FOR TODAY:

....

....

....

....

....

....

God blesses the one who reads the words of this
prophecy to the church, and he blesses all who
listen to its message and obey what it says.

REVELATION 1:3

Date:

MY MEMORY VERSE FOR TODAY:

....

....

....

....

....

THIS VERSE IS IMPORTANT TO REMEMBER BECAUSE. . .

....

....

....

....

....

WHAT IT MEANS TO MY FAITH:

....

....

....

....

....

HOW IT APPLIES TO MY LIFE:

....

....

....

....

KNOWING THIS VERSE WILL BE HELPFUL WHEN. . .

....

....

....

....

....

MY PRAYER FOR TODAY:

....

....

....

....

....

....

Fear of the Lord is the foundation of true wisdom.
All who obey his commandments will grow
in wisdom. Praise him forever!

PSALM 111:10

Date:

MY MEMORY VERSE FOR TODAY:

....

....

....

....

....

THIS VERSE IS IMPORTANT TO REMEMBER BECAUSE. . .

....

....

....

....

....

WHAT IT MEANS TO MY FAITH:

....

....

....

....

....

KNOWING THIS VERSE WILL BE HELPFUL WHEN. . .

MY PRAYER FOR TODAY:

*"And you will know the truth,
and the truth will set you free."*

JOHN 8:32

Date:

MY MEMORY VERSE FOR TODAY:

....

....

....

....

....

THIS VERSE IS IMPORTANT TO REMEMBER BECAUSE. . .

....

....

....

....

....

WHAT IT MEANS TO MY FAITH:

....

....

....

....

....

HOW IT APPLIES TO MY LIFE:

....

....

....

....

KNOWING THIS VERSE WILL BE HELPFUL WHEN. . .

....

....

....

....

....

MY PRAYER FOR TODAY:

....

....

....

....

....

....

....

For I find my delight in your
commandments, which I love.
PSALM 119:47 ESV

MY MEMORY VERSE FOR TODAY:

....

....

....

....

....

THIS VERSE IS IMPORTANT TO REMEMBER BECAUSE. . .

....

....

....

....

....

WHAT IT MEANS TO MY FAITH:

....

....

....

....

....

HOW IT APPLIES TO MY LIFE:

....

....

....

....

KNOWING THIS VERSE WILL BE HELPFUL WHEN. . .

....

....

....

....

....

MY PRAYER FOR TODAY:

....

....

....

....

....

....

Joyful is the person who finds wisdom, the one who gains understanding. For wisdom is more profitable than silver, and her wages are better than gold.

PROVERBS 3:13–14

Date:

MY MEMORY VERSE FOR TODAY:

....
....
....
....
....

THIS VERSE IS IMPORTANT TO REMEMBER BECAUSE. . .

....
....
....
....
....

WHAT IT MEANS TO MY FAITH:

....
....
....
....

HOW IT APPLIES TO MY LIFE:

....

....

....

....

KNOWING THIS VERSE WILL BE HELPFUL WHEN. . .

....

....

....

....

....

MY PRAYER FOR TODAY:

....

....

....

....

....

....

....

*"The Scripture you've just heard
has been fulfilled this very day!"*

LUKE 4:21

Date:

MY MEMORY VERSE FOR TODAY:

....

....

....

....

....

THIS VERSE IS IMPORTANT TO REMEMBER BECAUSE. . .

....

....

....

....

....

WHAT IT MEANS TO MY FAITH:

....

....

....

....

....

HOW IT APPLIES TO MY LIFE:

....

....

....

....

KNOWING THIS VERSE WILL BE HELPFUL WHEN. . .

....

....

....

....

....

MY PRAYER FOR TODAY:

....

....

....

....

....

....

....

*"This is all happening to fulfill the words of
the prophets as recorded in the Scriptures."*

MATTHEW 26:56

Date:

MY MEMORY VERSE FOR TODAY:

....
....
....
....
....

THIS VERSE IS IMPORTANT TO REMEMBER BECAUSE. . .

....
....
....
....
....

WHAT IT MEANS TO MY FAITH:

....
....
....
....
....

HOW IT APPLIES TO MY LIFE:

....

....

....

....

KNOWING THIS VERSE WILL BE HELPFUL WHEN. . .

....

....

....

....

....

MY PRAYER FOR TODAY:

....

....

....

....

....

....

....

Your love, GOD, fills the earth!
Train me to live by your counsel.
PSALM 119:64 MSG

Date:

MY MEMORY VERSE FOR TODAY:

....
....
....
....
....

THIS VERSE IS IMPORTANT TO REMEMBER BECAUSE. . .

....
....
....
....
....

WHAT IT MEANS TO MY FAITH:

....
....
....
....
....

HOW IT APPLIES TO MY LIFE:

....

....

....

....

KNOWING THIS VERSE WILL BE HELPFUL WHEN. . .

....

....

....

....

....

MY PRAYER FOR TODAY:

....

....

....

....

....

....

*Like newborn babies, you must crave pure spiritual
milk so that you will grow into a full experience
of salvation. Cry out for this nourishment.*

1 PETER 2:2

Date:

MY MEMORY VERSE FOR TODAY:

....

....

....

....

....

THIS VERSE IS IMPORTANT TO REMEMBER BECAUSE. . .

....

....

....

....

....

WHAT IT MEANS TO MY FAITH:

....

....

....

....

....

HOW IT APPLIES TO MY LIFE:

....

....

....

....

KNOWING THIS VERSE WILL BE HELPFUL WHEN. . .

....

....

....

....

....

MY PRAYER FOR TODAY:

....

....

....

....

....

....

*I passed on to you what was most important and
what had also been passed on to me. Christ
died for our sins, just as the Scriptures said.*

1 CORINTHIANS 15:3

Date:

MY MEMORY VERSE FOR TODAY:

....

....

....

....

....

THIS VERSE IS IMPORTANT TO REMEMBER BECAUSE. . .

....

....

....

....

....

WHAT IT MEANS TO MY FAITH:

....

....

....

....

....

KNOWING THIS VERSE WILL BE HELPFUL WHEN. . .

MY PRAYER FOR TODAY:

God, you did everything you promised, and I'm thanking you with all my heart. You pulled me from the brink of death, my feet from the cliff-edge of doom. Now I stroll at leisure with God in the sunlit fields of life.

PSALM 56:12–13 MSG

Date:

MY MEMORY VERSE FOR TODAY:

....
....
....
....
....

THIS VERSE IS IMPORTANT TO REMEMBER BECAUSE. . .

....
....
....
....
....

WHAT IT MEANS TO MY FAITH:

....
....
....
....
....

HOW IT APPLIES TO MY LIFE:

....

....

....

....

KNOWING THIS VERSE WILL BE HELPFUL WHEN. . .

....

....

....

....

....

MY PRAYER FOR TODAY:

....

....

....

....

....

....

....

"But if you remain in me and my words remain in you,
you may ask for anything you want, and it will be granted!"

JOHN 15:7

Date:

MY MEMORY VERSE FOR TODAY:

....

....

....

....

....

THIS VERSE IS IMPORTANT TO REMEMBER BECAUSE. . .

....

....

....

....

....

WHAT IT MEANS TO MY FAITH:

....

....

....

....

....

HOW IT APPLIES TO MY LIFE:

....

....

....

....

KNOWING THIS VERSE WILL BE HELPFUL WHEN. . .

....

....

....

....

....

MY PRAYER FOR TODAY:

....

....

....

....

....

....

....

*They have made God's law their own,
so they will never slip from his path.*

PSALM 37:31

Date:

MY MEMORY VERSE FOR TODAY:

....

....

....

....

....

THIS VERSE IS IMPORTANT TO REMEMBER BECAUSE. . .

....

....

....

....

....

WHAT IT MEANS TO MY FAITH:

....

....

....

....

....

HOW IT APPLIES TO MY LIFE:

KNOWING THIS VERSE WILL BE HELPFUL WHEN. . .

MY PRAYER FOR TODAY:

But be doers of the word,
and not hearers only.

JAMES 1:22 ESV

Date:

MY MEMORY VERSE FOR TODAY:

....

....

....

....

....

THIS VERSE IS IMPORTANT TO REMEMBER BECAUSE. . .

....

....

....

....

....

WHAT IT MEANS TO MY FAITH:

....

....

....

....

....

HOW IT APPLIES TO MY LIFE:

....

....

....

....

KNOWING THIS VERSE WILL BE HELPFUL WHEN. . .

....

....

....

....

....

MY PRAYER FOR TODAY:

....

....

....

....

....

....

Such things were written in the Scriptures long ago to teach
us. And the Scriptures give us hope and encouragement
as we wait patiently for God's promises to be fulfilled.

ROMANS 15:4

Date:

MY MEMORY VERSE FOR TODAY:

....

....

....

....

....

THIS VERSE IS IMPORTANT TO REMEMBER BECAUSE. . .

....

....

....

....

....

WHAT IT MEANS TO MY FAITH:

....

....

....

....

....

HOW IT APPLIES TO MY LIFE:

....

....

....

....

KNOWING THIS VERSE WILL BE HELPFUL WHEN. . .

....

....

....

....

....

MY PRAYER FOR TODAY:

....

....

....

....

....

....

*Above all, you must realize that no prophecy in
Scripture ever came from the prophet's own understanding,
or from human initiative. No, those prophets were
moved by the Holy Spirit, and they spoke from God.*

2 PETER 1:20–21

Date:

MY MEMORY VERSE FOR TODAY:

....
....
....
....
....

THIS VERSE IS IMPORTANT TO REMEMBER BECAUSE. . .

....
....
....
....
....

WHAT IT MEANS TO MY FAITH:

....
....
....
....
....

HOW IT APPLIES TO MY LIFE:

....

....

....

....

KNOWING THIS VERSE WILL BE HELPFUL WHEN. . .

....

....

....

....

....

MY PRAYER FOR TODAY:

....

....

....

....

....

....

*Each day the LORD pours his unfailing love
upon me, and through each night I sing his
songs, praying to God who gives me life.*

PSALM 42:8

Date:

MY MEMORY VERSE FOR TODAY:

....

....

....

....

....

THIS VERSE IS IMPORTANT TO REMEMBER BECAUSE. . .

....

....

....

....

....

WHAT IT MEANS TO MY FAITH:

....

....

....

....

HOW IT APPLIES TO MY LIFE:

....

....

....

....

KNOWING THIS VERSE WILL BE HELPFUL WHEN. . .

....

....

....

....

....

MY PRAYER FOR TODAY:

....

....

....

....

....

....

....

*Every word of God proves true. He is a
shield to all who come to him for protection.*

PROVERBS 30:5

GREAT SCRIPTURES TO MEMORIZE!

Don't know where to begin with your scripture memorization? Check out the following suggested memory verses.

1. Genesis 1:27
2. Exodus 14:14
3. Leviticus 19:18
4. Numbers 23:19
5. Deuteronomy 6:4–5
6. Joshua 1:8
7. Judges 3:9
8. Ruth 2:12
9. 1 Samuel 16:7
10. 2 Samuel 7:22
11. 1 Kings 2:3
12. 2 Kings 20:5
13. 1 Chronicles 16:11
14. 1 Chronicles 29:17
15. 2 Chronicles 7:14
16. 2 Chronicles 12:14
17. 2 Chronicles 15:7
18. Ezra 8:22
19. Nehemiah 8:10
20. Esther 4:14
21. Job 19:25
22. Psalm 27:1

IF YOU LOVED *THE SCRIPTURE MEMORY MAP FOR WOMEN*, YOU'LL ALSO LOVE. . .

The Prayer Map for Women

This engaging prayer journal is a fun and creative way for you to more fully experience the power of prayer in your life. Each page features a lovely 2-color design that guides you to write out specific thoughts, ideas, and lists. . .which then creates a specific "map" for you to follow as you talk to God.

Spiral Bound / 978-1-68322-557-7 / $7.99

The Bible Study Map for Women
(Available November 2019)

This unique journal is an engaging and creative way for you to dig deep into God's Word. Every colorful page will guide you to create your very own Bible study map as you write out specific thoughts, ideas, questions, and more which you can follow—from start to finish!—as you study God's Word.

Spiral Bound / 978-1-64352-178-7 / $7.99

DON'T MISS. . .

3-Minute Devotions for Women

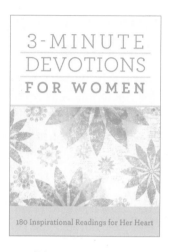

Take time to pause, reflect, and rejuvenate by reading
scripture, encouraging words, and a prayer starter to
begin a dialogue with God. No matter what your day
brings, this just-right-sized inspiration is guaranteed
to be the pick-me-up you need in your faith walk.

Paperback / 978-1-62029-735-3 / $4.99